Michael Hayes

24 Short Piano Pieces in All Keys

Intermediate Piano

To Young. You are the love of my life.

Special thanks to Wanda Cantrell and Reinhardt University.

Cover art and design by Diana Powell.
Sunset over the San Andres mountains during fire season.

ISBN 979-8-218-16287-0
ISBN 979-8-377-92130-1

CONTENTS

Peculiar Circumstance

By MICHAEL HAYES

Peculiar Circumstance 2 - 1

Peculiar Circumstance 2 - 2

Lonely House

By MICHAEL HAYES

For The Brave and Innocent

By MICHAEL HAYES

For The Brave and Innocent 2 - 1

For The Brave and Innocent 2 - 2

Conundrum

By MICHAEL HAYES

Conundrum 2 - 1

Comfort

By MICHAEL HAYES

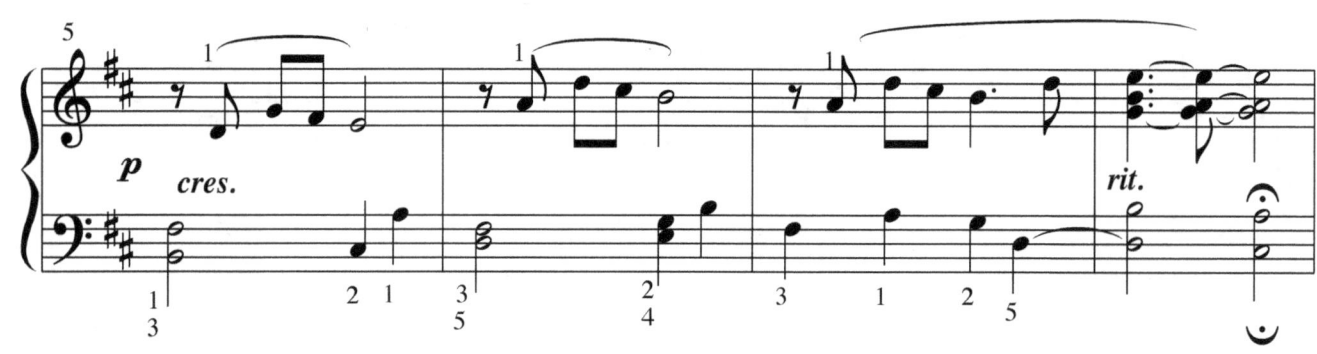

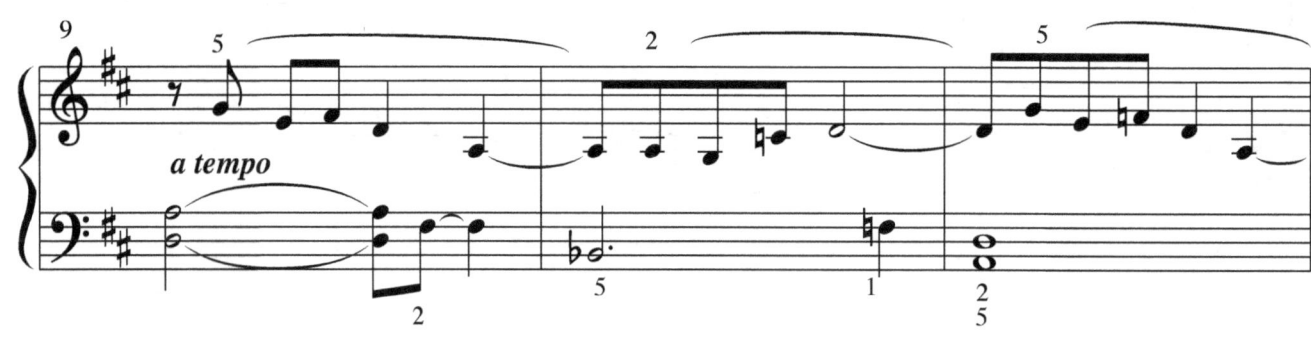

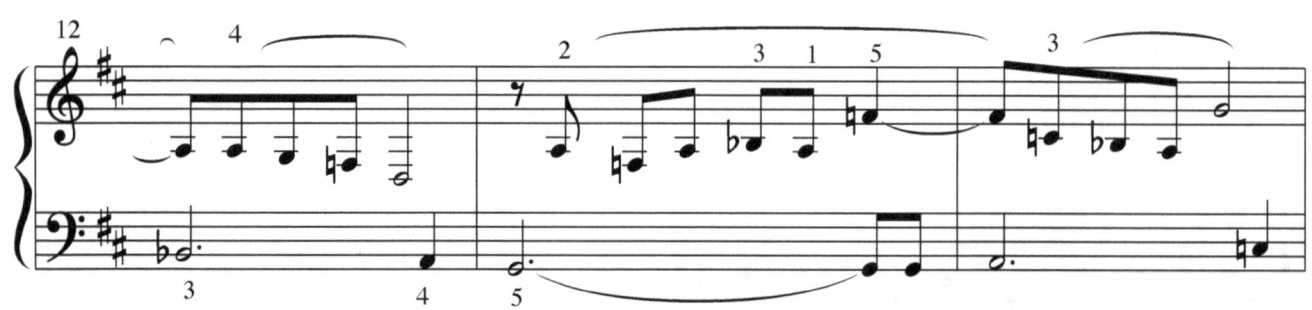

Comfort 2 - 1

Daydream

By MICHAEL HAYES

Daydream 2 - 2

Tenderness

By MICHAEL HAYES

Tears In The Snow

By MICHAEL HAYES

Tears in the Snow 2 - 1

Tears in the Snow 2 - 2

To Soar

By MICHAEL HAYES

To Soar 2 - 2

Seabirds

By MICHAEL HAYES

Sun On My Face

By MICHAEL HAYES

Sun On My Face 2 - 2

A Deep Sorrow

By MICHAEL HAYES

A Deep Sorrow 2 - 1

A Deep Sorrow 2 - 2

Bliss

By MICHAEL HAYES

(the glissando can be played with 5 fingers but will sound better is played with other technique)

D.C. al Coda

Coda

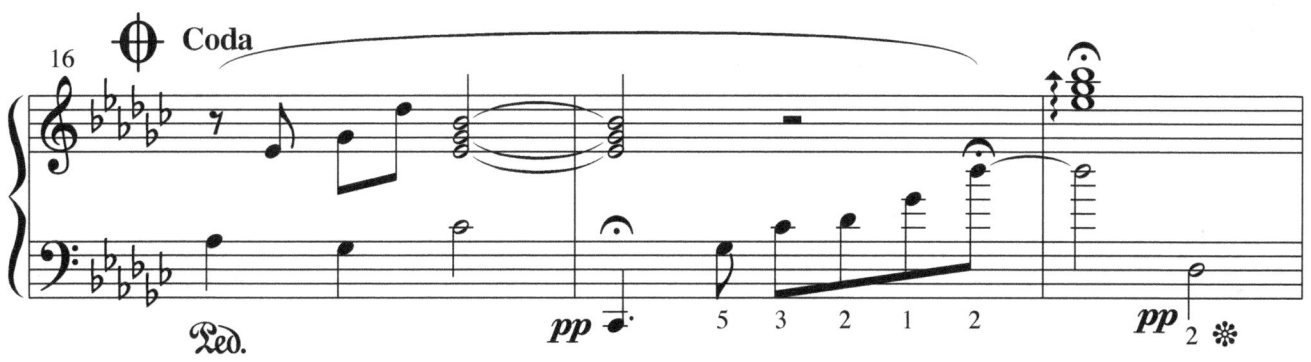

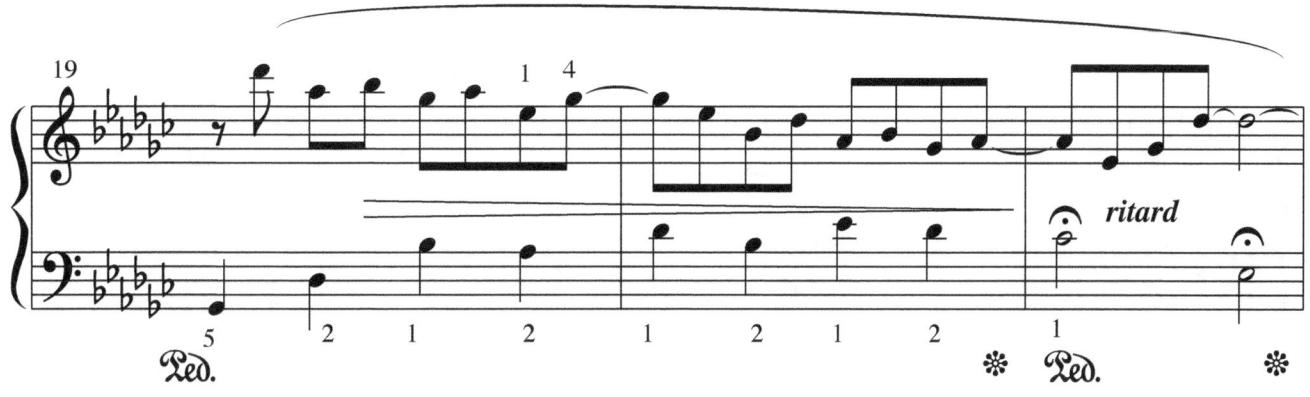

gliss.

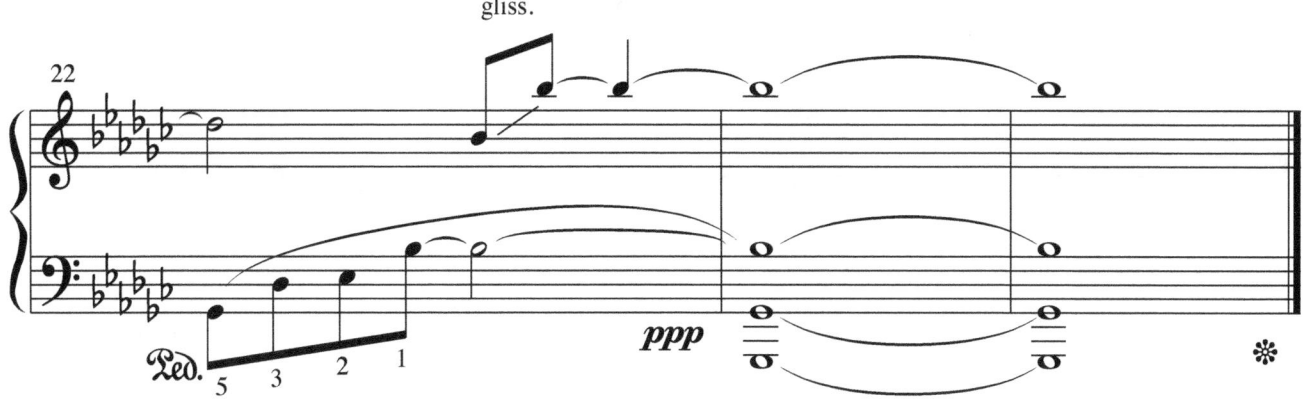

Argentina

By MICHAEL HAYES

Something Borrowed

By MICHAEL HAYES

Haunted Castle

By MICHAEL HAYES

♩=66
Spooky and mysterious

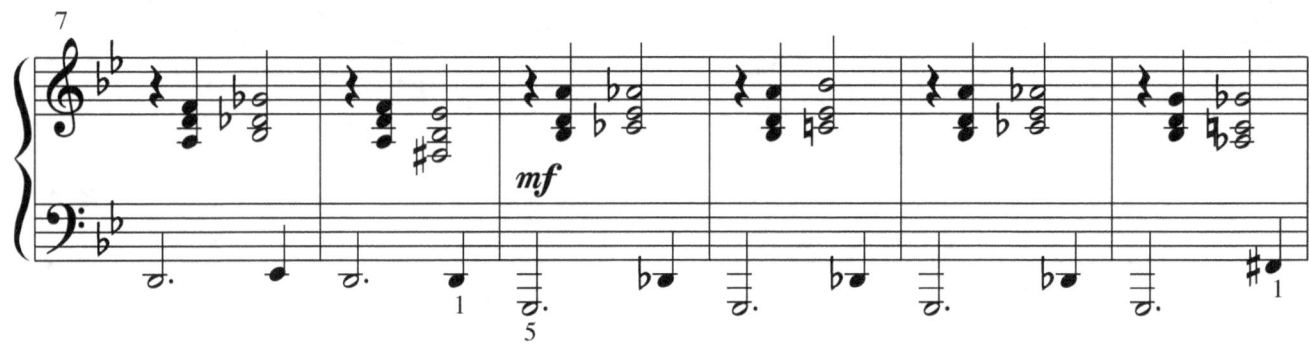

Haunted Castle 2 - 1

West Sky Morning

By MICHAEL HAYES

West Sky Morning 2 - 1

D. S. al Coda

Coda

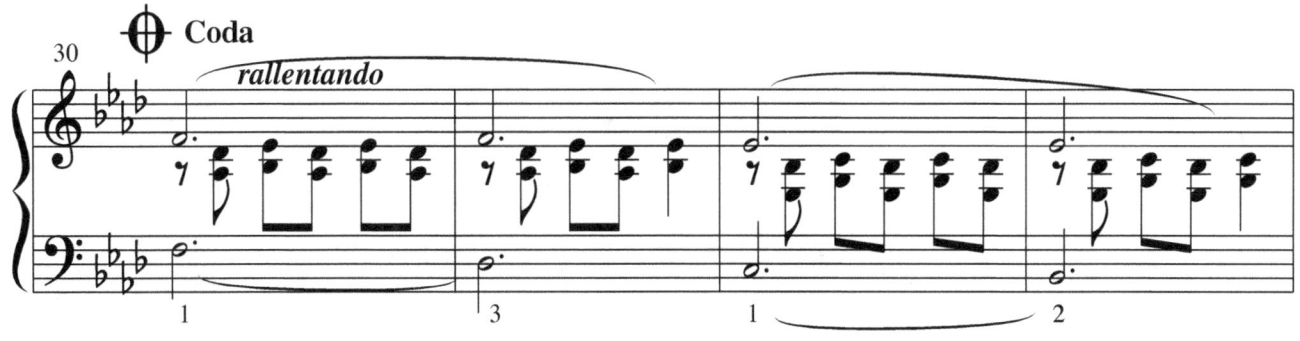

West Sky Morning 2 - 2

Mirror Mirror

By MICHAEL HAYES

Mirror Mirror 2 - 2

Calming Waters

By MICHAEL HAYES

At Peace 2 - 1

Reflective Mood

By MICHAEL HAYES

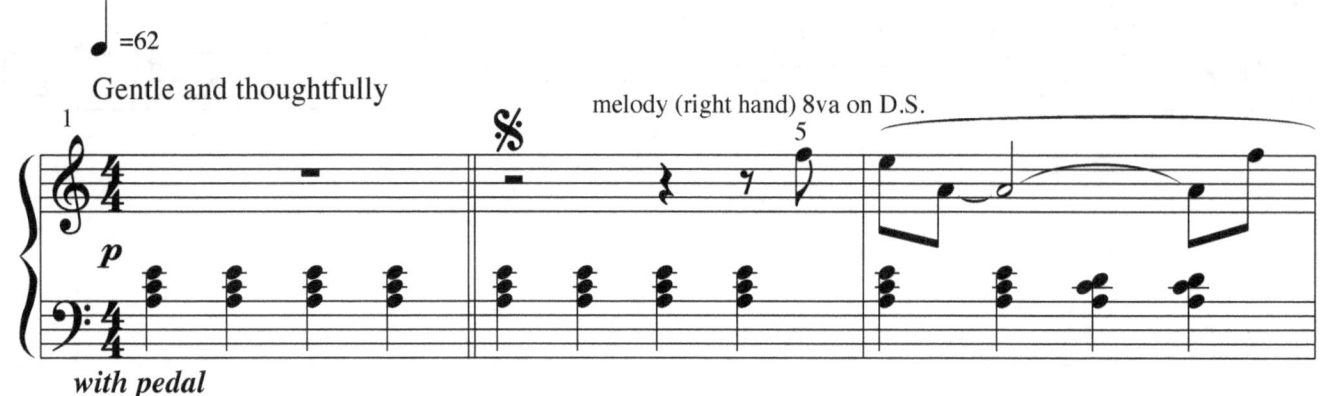

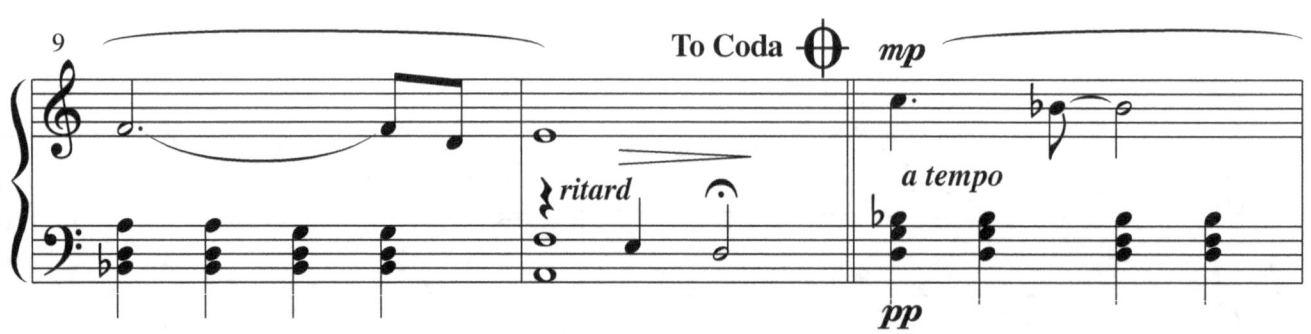

Reflective Mood 2 - 1

D.S. al Coda

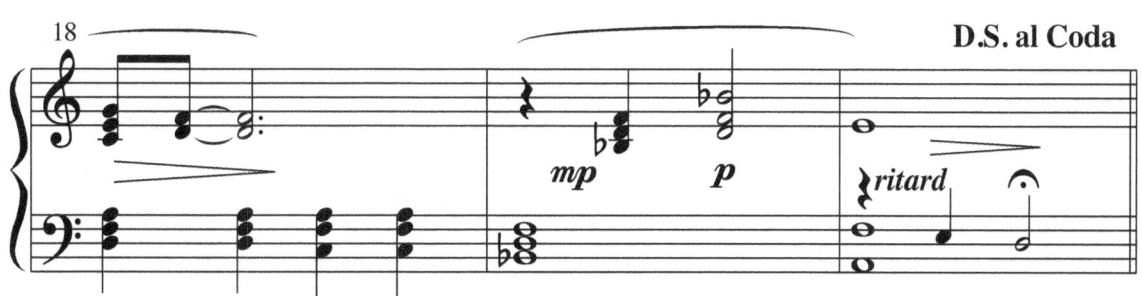

Coda

Ballerina

By MICHAEL HAYES

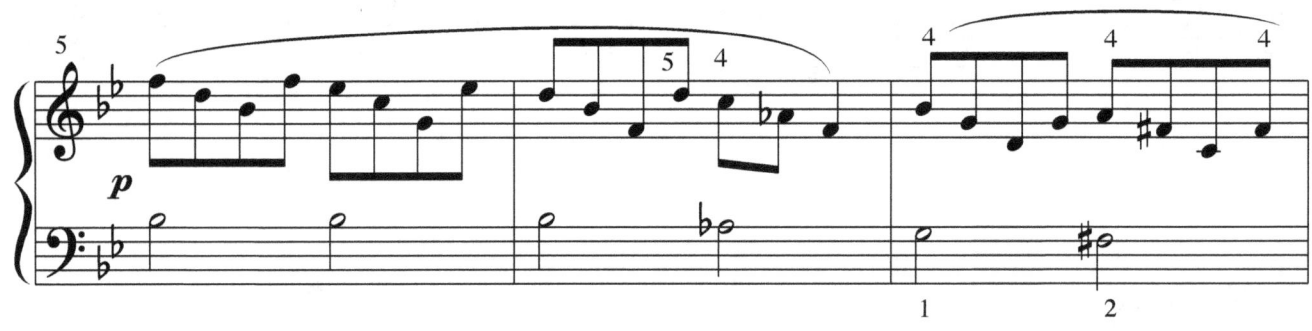

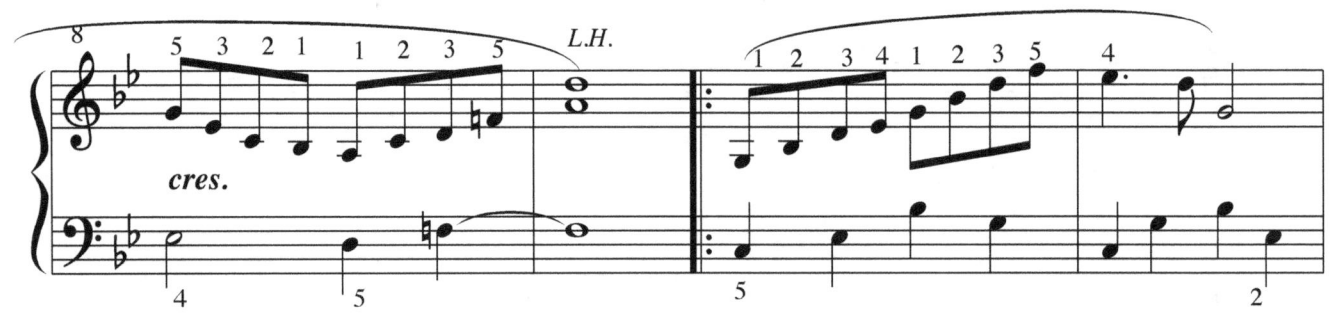

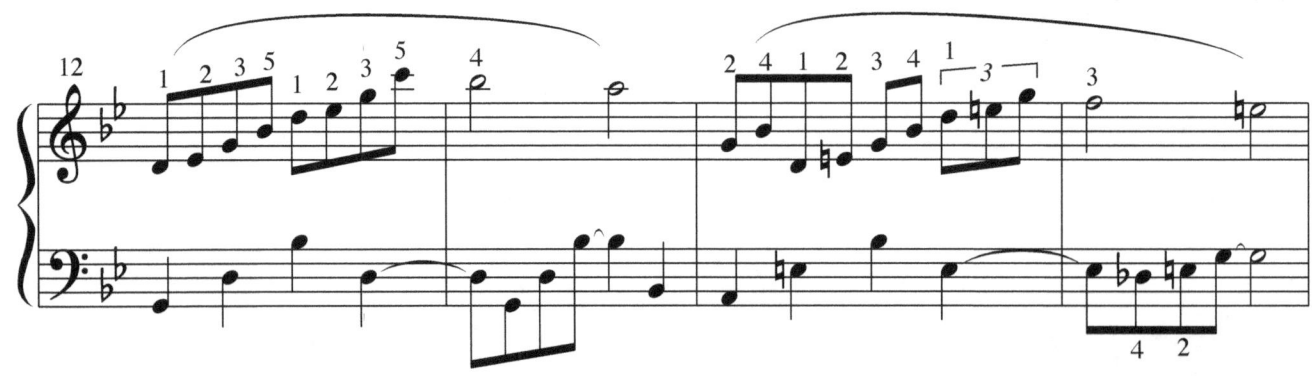

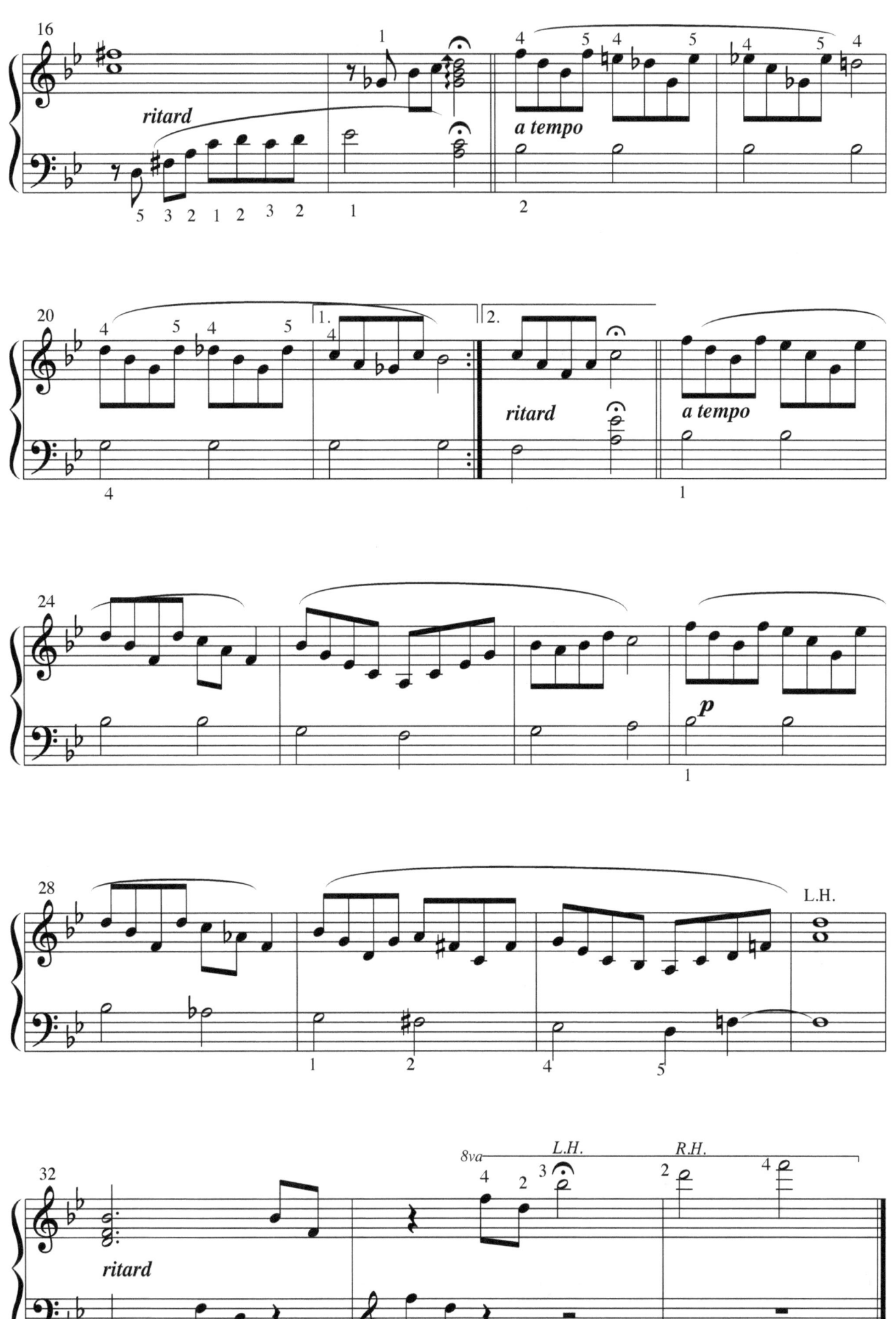

Ballerina 2 - 2

Fading Tears

By MICHAEL HAYES

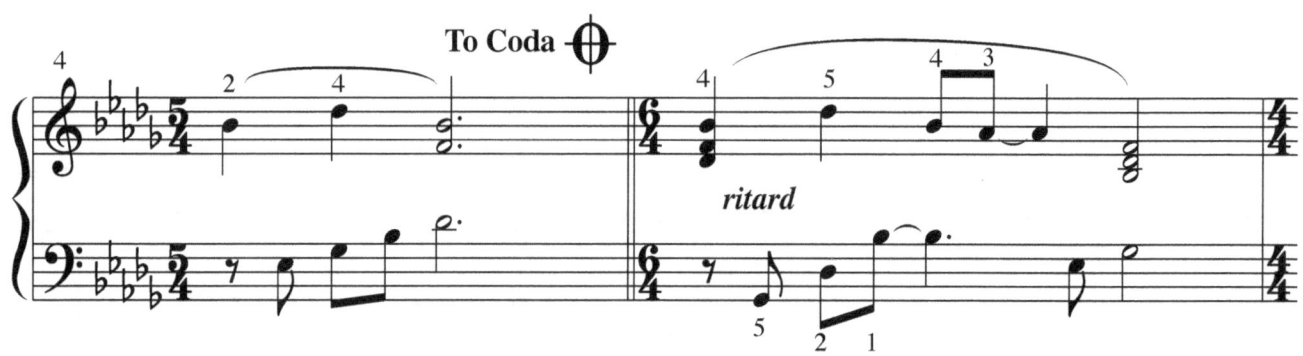

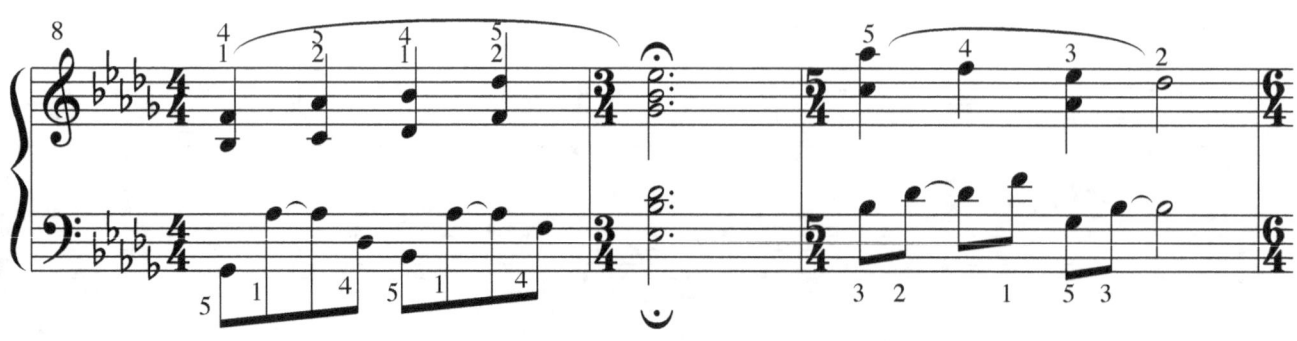

Fading Tears 2 - 1

D.C. al Coda

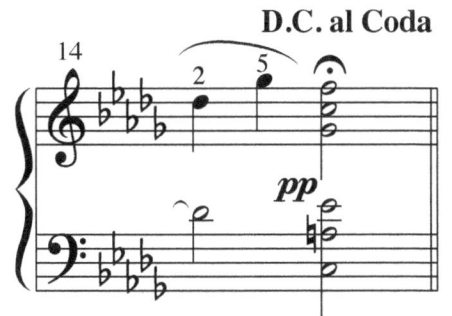

Coda

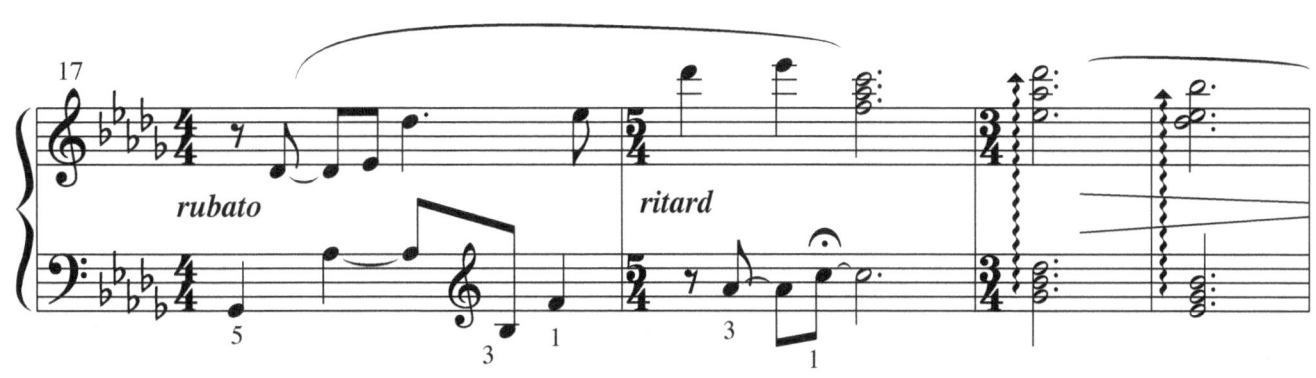

Fading Tears 2 - 2

Looking Up At Stars

By MICHAEL HAYES

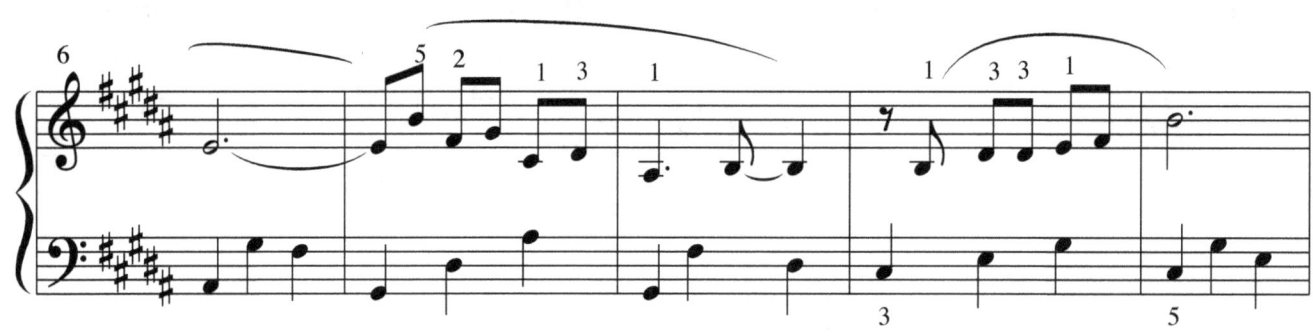

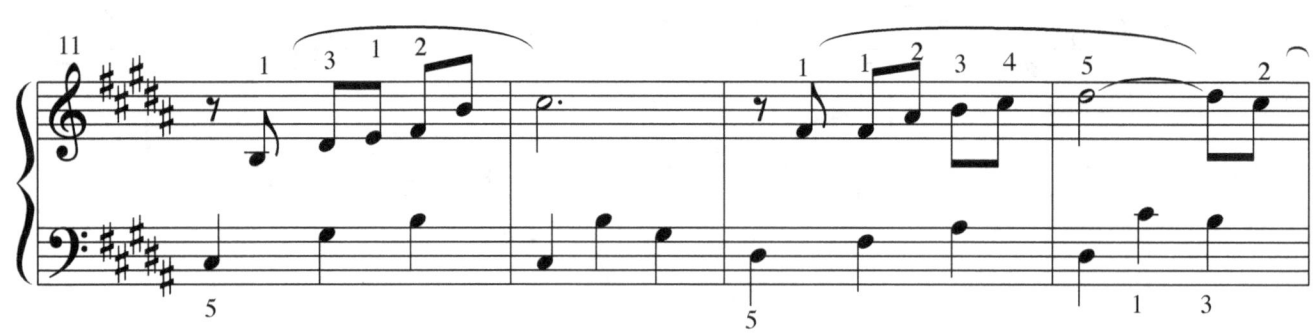

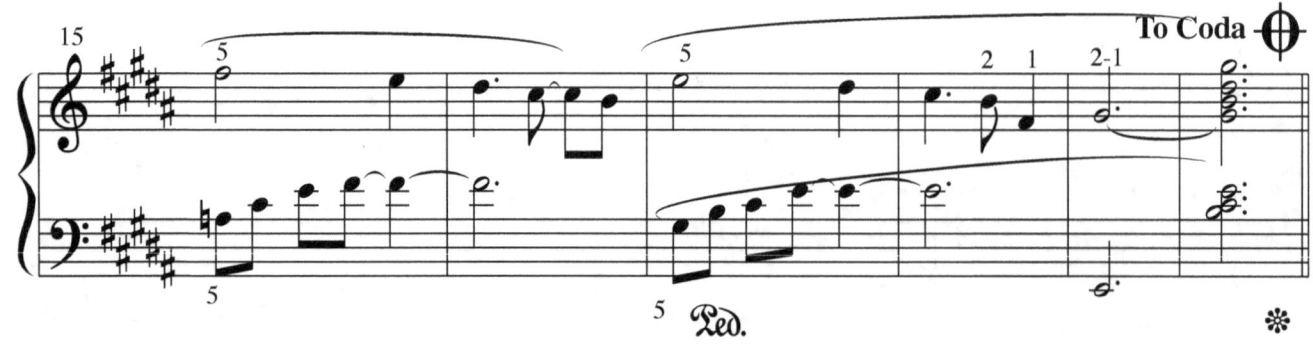

Looking Up At Stars 2 - 1

Looking Up At Stars 2 - 2

Contemplation

By MICHAEL HAYES

A WORD FROM THE COMPOSER

I have always had a desire to create. As a child, I built furniture from my father's leftover wood scraps and spent hours drawing and painting. As a teenager, I began playing guitar and writing songs and learned the drafting arts. In college, I enjoyed writing essays and papers. As an adult, I became a successful software designer. If it was a creative process, I enjoyed it.

I fell in love with music long ago. In part because my father led singing at my childhood church. In part, when we visited my Aunt, I would spend hours in front of her phonograph player listening to Rimsky-Korsokav's Scheherazade. It was a magical experience. I intended to major in music when I attended college, but I made other career choices.

I have not pursued music studies to the extent I could have. I haphazardly dabbled with whatever interested me at the moment. I played in bands, wrote songs, and learned guitar, piano, and cello. I achieved an intermediate level with these instruments but never became an expert with any.

Writing this collection has been a challenge, a labor of love. It is thrilling to hear the notes and harmonization of a new melody come together. Most importantly, it has allowed me to exercise my creative yearnings.

I probably work much harder than talented composers and musicians. At times I felt this project was too much, yet I persevered. The reward for my labor is the satisfaction of creating these 24 pieces. I hope the result is pleasing for those who undertake to play them, and I thank you.

The goal for this project was to write 24 pieces, one in each of the 24 keys, and limit each to two pages. Writing in all 24 keys was liberating and forced thinking in new ways. Each musical key seems to have its personality and flavor. The predefined constraints of two pages forced me to be better focused.

I love all types of music, classical, jazz, cinematic, new age, etc., and made no conscious attempt to imitate any style. I experimented and mixed ideas until they sounded pleasant. I sometimes followed the rules of theory and other times threw them out or was altogether unaware of the rules.

Like many individuals, I'd love to be a virtuoso on the piano, but I'm not. My favorite teachers I've encountered on my journey encouraged me to be original and not compare myself to others. I've tried to follow this great advice in all aspects of my life.

You are encouraged to make the music your own. Take liberties and experiment with the music. The tempo and other musical markings are merely suggestions. If you feel a different interpretation, then follow your muse. You are also encouraged to experiment, embellish, and ad-lib. It is your performance.

ACKNOWLEDGMENTS

I dedicate this work with love and appreciation to my wife, Young. You are best friend, my inspiration, my partner, and my soulmate. Your unwavering belief sustained me through the long hours of writing and revising. Your constant love and support inspire me to be the best version of myself.

To Wanda Cantrell, thank you for your patient, thoughtful, and detailed review. It has helped me tremendously in refining the pieces. Your performance was a true testament to your talent and passion. You breathed life into the music.

To my cello instructor, Deidre Emerson, for introducing me to Dr. Olga Harris of Tennessee State University. And to Dr. Harris for recommending I compose some 2-page pieces. Your suggestion was the catalyst for this collection.

To Diana Powell, thank you for your beautiful photography and cover design. It is a stunning visual representation that perfectly captures the spirit of the music. See more of Diana's exquisite work at https://fineartamerica.com/profiles/diana-powell.

To Laurie Cline, for proofreading my text. Your keen eye for detail and expertise was priceless. Laurie is the author of Counting It All Joy: Choosing Joy over Painful Circumstances with God's Help on Amazon.

To all my musical friends: Bob Bowman, Jim Cremeens, Roger Daniell, Stephen Davis, Danny Hogan, Jeff Keen, Shelby Lock, Steve Lockwood, Todd Lockwood, Ken Musselman, Larry Pilon, Buffy Rhea, Gary Riley, Tim Sauder, Bob Stewart, and Rick Vigelt. Thank you all for being part of my journey.

In loving memory of Rick Garber and Rick Stolp, you are greatly missed.

PERFORMANCE NOTES

The majority of the pieces are at a relaxed meditative tempo. They run between 1.5 and 2 minutes in length, depending on the chosen performance tempo. The longest is about 3 minutes and 20 seconds.

Mp3 file downloads are at www.earshockmusic.com/24pieces. The password for the download is 24sp.

Kindle eBook

To navigate to the page of a song title, click on the title in the table of contents. To return to the table of contents, click on the song title heading.

Metronome Markings

Metronome markings are only guidelines. They do not account for all musical elements contributing to the overall feel of a performance. Metronome markings help establish a general sense of tempo, but they are not strict mandates. The ultimate goal is to create expressive, engaging, and meaningful music. Play at a tempo that is comfortable and inspiring for you.

Rubato Usage

Rubato indications are often absent. You are encouraged to freely and artistically use rubato and interpret the music your way to make it unique and personal.

Tasteful use of rubato can create an emotional connection with your audience, helping them to understand and feel the music on a deeper level. Rubato gives you greater control over the dynamic elements. By slowing down or speeding up, you can shape the music to suit the mood and character of the piece.

A word of warning, overuse can be detracting and make the performance seem uneven. Strive for a balance between expression and maintaining the overall structure and flow of the music.

Dynamic Markings

Just like metronome markings, the dynamic markings are just suggestions. It's up to you, the performer, to make the final decision on how to play the dynamics in a particular piece. Give priority to your interpretation and the individual performance style over any markings in the music.

Fermata Markings

Treat fermata (hold) markings as suggestions. Use your interpretation of the music. Experiment with the amount of time devoted to a hold. Some will feel better applying a short time interval, while others may suggest a longer time.

Repeat Markings

Repeat markings are suggestions rather than strict instructions. I leave it to the performer's choice to perform the repeats or play a section only once.

The same applies to "DC al Coda" (Da Capo al Coda) and "DS al Coda" (Dal Segno al Coda) repeat symbols. Skipping these repeats and jumping directly to the coda, at times, is acceptable. Use your musical ear when making these choices.

Once familiar with a piece, you may find an alternative way to create repeat sections of your choosing. Use your musical judgment to make these choices.

Pedaling

"With pedal" is indicated at the beginning of all pieces. Excessive sustain pedal use produces a murky unclear sound (pedal blur), so it's best to pedal in moderation. Applying the pedal at chord changes yields good results.

When writing for piano, sustained notes in the left-hand chords can make the score appear messy with numerous tied notes. At times sustaining arpeggiated chords with the fingers instead of the sustain pedal will yield a better result. Strive for this when possible.

Pedal markings appear in a few locations. These locations, in my opinion, work well. However, as always, use your judgment.

Symbols/Markings

   Pedal down

   Pedal up

Treble clef one octave higher than written

   Treble clef one octave lower than written

   Bass clef one octave lower than written

Peculiar Circumstance – With an uncertain attitude

"Peculiar Circumstance" is a piece that tells the story of an unusual and unexpected event. Deviation from the center tonality of C major gives this piece its sense of uncertainty and mystique, a peculiar circumstance.

Enjoy playing with the chromatic notes outside of the C major tonality. These chromatic notes add rich layers of color, contributing to its feeling of uncertainty and adding depth and interest to the piece.

Lonely House – Mysterious and lonely

"Lonely House" is a simple piece reflecting a sense of loneliness and solitude. The music echoes the fear and unease of abandonment.

This house is old and mysterious and has a feeling of sadness. It is on the verge of becoming haunted. Midway, the mood changes to one of reflection, becoming more introspective. Feel the memories and emotions the house has within its walls.

For The Brave and Innocent – With solemn respect

"For The Brave and Innocent" expresses honor and reverence for those who have sacrificed themselves and for the innocent victims of any tragic event. The piece is simple and elegant. It is a touching tribute to those who have made the ultimate sacrifice and a reminder of the power of selflessness and bravery.

Play with reverence and respect. Be delicate and tender to capture the purity and gentleness of the innocent victims. If you know someone, make a dedication with your performance. When playing the melody of Taps in the last 3 bars, think of how it would sound at a funeral.

Conundrum – Mysteriously

A conundrum is a puzzle that is complex and challenging. "Conundrum" uses minimal elements to create this sense of complexity and uncertainty.

The statement of the puzzle is a simple repetitive melody. At bar 13, the tension builds in the puzzle melody. Think of a mystery movie where the detective confronts a brain-teaser problem.

Comfort – Peaceful and at rest

"Comfort" is a simple piece meant to evoke a feeling of comfort and relaxation in the listener.

This piece opens with a soft, gentle melody, creating a sense of calm and stillness. Think of a meditative state of peaceful happiness. Play with expression, conveying the mood and emotion of the music through your playing. Try to bring a sense of peace and serenity to listeners.

Daydream – With dreamlike quality

"Daydream" is about the emotions and thoughts arising when daydreaming. It aims to evoke feelings of being lost in thought and exploring the inner self.

Allow yourself to drift to a personal reflective place, taking a gentle and peaceful ride through your imagination. Let your mind create a private world. Employ the power and the beauty of allowing one's mind to wander and reflect.

Is your daydream sitting on a beach or under a shade tree? Do you travel someplace? Are you alone or with other people? There are no rules. Your daydream is your own.

Tenderness – Affectionately

"Tenderness" is a heartfelt, affectionate message to a special someone. Throughout the piece, the mood should remain gentle and serene, focused on creating a sense of intimacy and tenderness between the listener and the music. At the end of the piece, leave the listener feeling warm and comfortable.

Tears In The Snow – Soft, sad, with feeling

"Tears in the Snow" is an emotional piece that captures feelings of sadness and introspection accompanying the coming of winter. The contrast between the cold snow and warm emotional tears creates a powerful image of sadness and loss amidst the serene beauty of winter.

The overall mood should remain sad and reflective. The piece ends with the tempo slowing down as the melody becomes simpler. Hear the sound of the last flurries of snow blowing away.

With your performance, picture the scene: It's a winter's day with snow falling softly from the sky, creating a serene and peaceful atmosphere. The ground is a blanket of pristine snow. Amid the peaceful winter wonderland, you see a single teardrop fall to the snow. The teardrop's path down the person's cheek is visible, tracing a line through the snowflakes that have landed on their face.

In bar 42, the treble clef with the number 8 on top indicates to play the part one octave higher.

To Soar – With a free spirit

"To Soar" is a beautiful and uplifting piece with feelings of flying and floating high in the sky. The steady rhythm creates a feeling of smooth flight. Legato playing will add fluidity and a sense of effortless soaring. The repeats and decrescendo starting at the Coda, slowly bring the listener back to earth with a peaceful and calming conclusion.

Seabirds – Lively and fun

"Seabirds" starts with soft arpeggios and a melodic theme representing the gentle movements of seabirds as they glide over the waves. Play with a delicate touch to suggest the grace and beauty of the birds in flight.

The downward runs at bar 23 reflect a sudden burst of flapping wings and the powerful flight of the seabirds. Let your performance bring the majesty of these creatures to life and evoke feelings of wonder.

Sun On My Face – With happiness and joy

"Sun On My Face" is a cheerful and lighthearted composition evoking the feeling of basking in the warm sun. The mood begins cheerfully but occasionally becomes slightly contemplative as clouds pass over the sun.

The A section begins with simple Mozarteque broken chord figures. The B section, starting at bar 23, becomes more challenging. Try to bring out the last two eighth notes of each bar. This section could be the partly cloudy part of the day.

A Deep Sorrow – Slow and mournful

"A Deep Sorrow" is a piece characterizing the emotions of grief and despair. The music is slow and deliberately paced, with each note portraying a heavy heart. The simple yet poignant melody repeats a mournful tune that tugs at the listener's heartstrings. As the piece progresses, the mood becomes increasingly intense with dissonant rich, complex harmonies.

A friend told me this piece reminded them of Queen Elizabeth II's funeral. This lament truly expresses the mourning and grief appropriate of a funeral dirge.

Bliss – Freely

"Bliss" has an improvisational quality exploring different ideas and sounds (e.g., the glissandi in bars 9 to 12). Try to create a sense of happiness, free from the burdens of everyday life. Feel the relaxation and contentment that transcend everyday experiences. Take the listener on a journey that sinks into the peaceful and calming atmosphere you create. Okay, maybe that's a little deep, but you get the idea.

Here are some suggestions for executing the glissandi.

All glissandi move from lower to higher notes. Execute them with a technique comfortable for you.

A technique of all five fingers in a rolling motion can play bars 9 through 12. The glissandi will sound better with a sweeping motion of the hand technique.

For bars 14 and 22, if you use the five-finger technique, experiment and decide what notes you should omit for a pleasing sound. Use the back of the fingers or the fleshy part of the thumb techniques to stop more accurately on the notes.

Argentina – with nostalgic longing

"Argentina" expresses memories and the longing to return to Argentina. The tango-inspired rhythmic pattern in the left hand supports a melancholy melody. There is a sense of yearning, perhaps for love left behind. Play slowly and expressively to produce a mood of nostalgic longing.

Something Borrowed – Gently

"Something Borrowed" begins with a simple melody and chord progression. The harmony gradually becomes more complex. The harmonic tensions create interest and a dynamic atmosphere.

In bar 9, the harmony expands a little more. In bars 13 through 15, the melody achieves the most tension before a return to a familiar consonance in bar 16. The melody reaches its height in bars 17 through 19 before returning to the beginning. The listener is thrown one last curve with the ending that begins in bar 22.

Haunted Castle – Spooky and mysterious

"Haunted Castle" starts with a slow eerie chordal melody evoking the ominous atmosphere of the old haunted castle. The steady chords and bass line, create a sense of suspense. Throughout the piece, careful use of dynamics will add to the overall eerie atmosphere.

As the piece progresses, the right-hand chords become more complex, harmonically dense, and agitated to add to the feeling of unease. Enjoy the spooky middle section in bars 22 through 31.

Watch out in bars 22 through 29, where the left hand changes to treble clef. Likewise, watch out in bar 37, where the right hand changes to bass clef.

West Sky Morning – Peaceful mountain morning

"West Sky Morning" is a peaceful, serene piece. It evokes the feeling of watching a sunrise over the western horizon. The sky changes color as daylight increases, transitioning from deep dark midnight blue to shades of orange and pink.

The arrangement starts with delicate chords in the upper register. The main melody begins at bar 5, played by the left hand. Dotted half notes in the right hand represent a slow-moving secondary melody.

In bar 17, the dotted half-notes switch from the little finger to the thumb. Try to sustain the dotted half notes.

If the broken chords are too challenging, try playing the piece using only blocked chords on quarter notes. After you are comfortable, transition to playing the broken chords.

The piece should be performed with a feeling of calm, serenity, and renewal, capturing the beauty and majesty of a West Sky Morning.

Mirror Mirror – Thoughtful and reminiscent

"Mirror Mirror" is a beautiful and contemplative exploration of self-reflection through a musical journey of emotions and introspection. The piece opens with a gentle and melancholic descending line followed by a repetitive melody, allowing the listener to focus on the sentiments it conveys.

Beginning in bar 5, the top note of the eighth note pairs is the melody, and the lower is the harmony. Try to highlight the top note. Release the sustain pedal frequently to avoid pedal blur.

Take a long hard look in the mirror for a moment of self-reflection. The piece should leave the listener with a sense of resolution and clarity as if the process of reflection has brought a new understanding.

Calming Waters – Calm and peaceful

"Calming Waters" features a relaxed tempo and soft, soothing harmonies. Picture yourself sitting with your feet in the water, relaxing on a hot day. It's a moment to slow down, breathe deeply, and let your thoughts wander, helping you to unwind and decompress.

This simple pleasure can help you connect with nature and take a break from the hustle and bustle of daily life. The image of serene surroundings can create a sense of tranquility and well-being. Play delicately with a focus on creating a peaceful atmosphere.

Reflective Mood – Gentle and thoughtfully

"Reflective Mood" is slow and gentle, with a sense of contemplation and peaceful introspection. It is somewhat Chopinesque of Prelude No. 4 from Opus 28.

The piece opens with soft, delicate chords that gradually build and fill the musical space, creating a sense of wonder and serenity. The melody is simple and unadorned, allowing the listener to immerse themselves and reflect on their feelings and thoughts.

Take time out for reflection. Play with a delicate touch and subtle variations in dynamics to convey emotions, from wistfulness to melancholy to hope.

The 8va on the melody is optional, your choice.

Ballerina – Enthusiastically

"Ballerina" is an enthusiastic, lively, and energetic piece about a young ballerina. It is a tribute to the magic of childhood and the beauty, energy, grace, and passion of a young performer.

The piece starts with an upbeat, cheerful, steady rhythm propelling the young ballerina toward her dreams and aspirations. There are two mood changes at bars 10 and 18, respectively.

Let your performance be bright and lively. You want the music to capture grace, elegance, and fluidity. Bring the dancer to life through the music.

Fading Tears – Sad and slow

"Fading Tears" is a haunting and evocative piece with a sense of sadness and longing. It is deeply emotional and captures the essence of heartbreak and sorrow.

The piece begins with a simple, sad melody played softly and expressively. Multiple time signature changes add complexity and sophistication.

The primary theme alternates time signatures 6/4 and 5/4 for the first four bars. Dotted half notes at the end of each of the first four bars serve as a musical representation of sadness and longing. These pauses permit the listener to experience the emotions the music is expressing.

Watch for bars 6 and 17, where the left hand changes to treble clef. Also, watch for the many time signature changes in the piece.

Don't rush the performance. Feel free to use lots of rubato. Give the listener time to absorb the sadness of each note.

Looking Up At Stars – Joyful but relaxed

"Looking Up at the Stars" evokes feelings of wonder and awe as one gazes at the endless beauty in the night sky. Imagine the setting of an open field and an atmosphere of spaciousness and serenity.

The piece begins with a soft, contemplative melody. Bars 21 through 29 use sustained chords in the left hand to create a feeling of spaciousness and distance. The ending, at the Coda, represents a shooting star and serves as a reminder of the incredible sights seen when one looks up at the stars. Playing the melody an octave higher on the repeat is optional.

Contemplation - Thoughtfully

"Contemplation" is a slow and meditative piece characterized by an introspective and reflective nature. The harmonies are simple and spacious, allowing moments of stillness and quiet contemplation with each chord change. The melody is slow and lyrical, emphasizing the mood of the piece.

The 9/8 time signature has a lilting and flowing feel. Subdividing the measures into three groups of three beats each gives the piece a triple-meter feeling. The slow tempo ensures each pulse is felt and adds to the meditative nature.

Depending on the listener's mood, the piece may evoke a feeling of sadness, solitude, or peace. Use your perspective for your interpretation of the piece.